GRAMPIAN'S LAST DAYS OF S

by

W.A.C. Smith

The Caledonian Railway prided itself on its timekeeping ('The True line') and the Strathmore route was one of its racing grounds. In 1937 the LMS introduced three hour schedules between Glasgow and Aberdeen, but heavy wartime traffic, followed by nationalisation, saw trains taking four hours or more to cover the 153 miles and timekeeping was poor. Of the 121 journeys I made over all or part of the route between 1950 and 1960 only 14% managed a punctual arrival, 1957 being the worst year with 146 minutes lost on thirteen journeys. However, in summer 1962 the service was recast and accelerated with class A4 Pacifics as the rostered motive power. Class A2 and A3 Pacifics and Black Five 4-6-0s, including the standard variant, were also used, and on 18 August 1962 I photographed class A3 No. 60094, 'Colorado', soon after its leaving Stonehaven with the 1.30 p.m. 'Grampian' from Aberdeen. The locomotive's name came from a racehorse, owned by Lord Derby, which was the winner of the 2,000 Guineas in 1926.

Text and photographs © W.A.C. Smith, 2005.
First published in the United Kingdom, 2005,
by Stenlake Publishing Ltd.
01290 551122
www.stenlake.co.uk

ISBN 9781840333398

Printed by
Blissetts, Roslin Road, Acton, W3 8DH

The legendary LNER Pacific 'Flying Scotsman', purchased privately for preservation following its withdrawal by British Railways in 1963, worked a special train from Edinburgh to Aberdeen for Queen's College Railway and Transport Society on 16 May 1964. I photographed it on the return journey, passing through Stonehaven Station hard on the heels of the 5.15 p.m. express from Aberdeen. In later years the locomotive toured the USA and Australia, and is now part of the National Collection housed in York Railway Museum.

INTRODUCTION

Grampian region comprises the counties of Aberdeen, Kincardine, Banff and Moray. In 1850 the Aberdeen Railway, striking north from Guthrie on the Arbroath & Forfar Railway, reached a temporary terminus at Ferryhill on the outskirts of the Granite City, and three years later the Deeside Railway was opened from Ferryhill to Banchory. In 1854 both companies extended their services to a new station at Guild Street in the city centre. Also in 1854 the Great North of Scotland Railway was opened between Kittybrewster, on the northern outskirts of Aberdeen, and Huntly. The Aberdeen Railway amalgamated with the Scotland Midland Junction Railway in 1856 to form the Scottish North Eastern Railway, which became part of the Caledonian Railway in 1866, and the Deeside Railway passed to the Great North of Scotland Railway in 1875.

In 1856 GNSR passenger services were extended from Kittybrewster over the bed of the former Aberdeenshire Canal to Waterloo Quay, and then, in 1867, the Denburn Valley line was opened from Kittybrewster to a new Joint station, shared with the Caledonian Railway (and, later, the North British Railway) and adjacent to the original Guild Street station which was retained for goods traffic.

The Great North company inaugurated suburban services (known locally as the 'Subbies') on Donside in 1887 and on Deeside in 1894, and a much needed rebuilding of Aberdeen Joint Station, with new signalling, additional platforms and the widening of the approach from Ferryhill, took place between 1907 and 1915, resulting in a station which, upon withdrawal of the suburban services in 1937 because of tram and bus competition, was to give an impression of an over abundance of facilities.

The Great North of Scotland eventually totalled 334 route miles, with a stock of 122 locomotives (predominately of the 4-4-0 wheel arrangement), 766 carriages and 3,603 wagons, comprising a main line from Aberdeen to Keith and Elgin and a network of branches, some lengthy, serving the north-east corner of Scotland. Today, only the main line from Aberdeen to Keith survives, connecting there with the former Highland Railway route to Elgin and Inverness.

The railway grouping of 1923 resulted in the Caledonian and Highland Railways becoming part of the West Coast Group (London, Midland &

Scottish Railway) with the North British and Great North of Scotland Railways going to the East Coast Group (London & North Eastern Railway). For the LNER to access Aberdeen required perpetuation of the North British Railway's running powers, dating from 1883, over the 38 miles of Caledonian (now LMS) metals from Kinnaber Junction, north of Montrose, but this anomaly was ended on 1 January 1948 when British Railways' Scottish Region came into being. Consequent upon closure of the Strathmore line in 1967, and Brechin branch in 1981, Kinnaber Junction no longer exists.

Steam working ended on the three hour expresses between Glasgow and Aberdeen in September 1966, while in the north east the last steam operated service was that on the Banff branch which was closed in July 1964.

My childhood was spent in Aberdeen and an early memory is of an exhibition of locomotives and rolling stock held at the Joint station in aid of hospital funds, exhibits including LNER Pacific No. 4472 'Flying Scotsman'. On another occasion the LMS 'Royal Scot' train which had toured America was put on show.

By 1938 we were occupying an eminently desirable residence with the Ballater branch at the bottom of the garden and an uninterrupted view of both Ferryhill locomotive shed and the main line south. The new, apple green P2 2-8-2s of the LNER were a familiar sight on Edinburgh expresses, having replaced former North British Atlantics, but one July morning I was greeted by the sight of the last of the Atlantics, No. 9875, 'Midlothian', simmering in the shed yard. It had been returned to service with a view to preservation which, unfortunately, was not to materialise because of the Second World War. Also in the summer of 1938 I saw an LMS Coronation Pacific not long

Right: Class WD 2-8-0 No. 90441 rattles through closed Portlethen Station on 16 May 1964 southbound from Aberdeen with empty wagons for the Fife coalfield. The station had been closed in 1956, but has been reopened for commuters.

out of Crewe Works and looking magnificent in its immaculate crimson lake livery.

It was about this time that I had my first ever footplate trip, admittedly only the length of Ferryhill shed yard, but a never-to-be-forgotten experience. The locomotive was an LNER class B12 4-6-0 which had come down from Kittybrewster shed to work a Wednesday half day excursion to Montrose. The B12s were former Great Eastern Railway locomotives, of a design dating back to 1911, twelve of which were eventually transferred to the Great North of Scotland section, commencing in 1931. Happy days indeed, when steam reigned supreme and the 'Big Four' railway companies were trendsetters not only in land transport, but also at sea and, with Railway Air Services, which operated internal flights, in the air!

However, six years of war followed by half a century of nationalisation have resulted in today's fragmented, quasi-privatised and heavily subsidised system. The future even of this seems increasingly uncertain in a country firmly wedded to the perceived flexibility of road transport, regardless of its horrendous accident statistics, pollution, damage to the environment and major contribution to global warming. One can only hope that the railway is not fated to join such forgotten forms of transport as the stagecoach, sailing ship, and airship.

On the gloriously sunny morning of 17 June 1962 veteran Caledonian 0-6-0 No. 57581 made a fine sight south of Cove Bay as it headed the 'Scottish Railtour' – most of the passengers were from south of the border – en route from Aberdeen to Forfar and covering several closed branch lines. The locomotive had been brought from Polmadie shed at Glasgow especially for the occasion.

Ferryhill Junction at Aberdeen, photographed on 16 June 1962 with A3 Pacific No. 60057, 'Ormonde', on a 7.23 p.m. relief train for King's Cross. The Ballater branch is on the left, while the entrance to Ferryhill shed is in the foreground. The container wagons on the right are in Denburn South sidings.

Normally all photographs used in the *Last Days of Steam* series have been taken by myself and are thus confined to the British Railways era, but I have pre-war memories of Aberdeen's railways (see Introduction) and particularly of Ferryhill locomotive shed where, on occasion, I persuaded my father to take photographs with the family box camera. One of these, taken *c*.1936, is reproduced here and shows LMS class 5XP Jubilee 4-6-0 No. 5584. Built in 1934 by the North British Locomotive Co. of Glasgow, the locomotive is shown in original condition. It was later named 'North West Frontier' and in 1948 became British Railways class 6P No. 45584. It was withdrawn from service in 1964.

Also taken *c.*1936 was this photograph of LNER class O4 2-8-0 No. 6290, flanked by a former North British 'Scott' on the left, and an LMS compound 4-4-0. I was later to find that No. 6290 had an interesting history, being one of a large batch of these locomotives, of a Great Central design dating from 1911, built during the First World War for overseas service with the Railway Operating Division of the Royal Engineers. Many were subsequently purchased by the LNER and No. 6290 came to Scotland in 1924 to haul coal from Fife to Aberdeen for the fleet of deep sea fishing trawlers which, in those days, were coal fired. During the Second World War, however, all the Scottish based locomotives of this class were transferred away.

Almost thirty years later, on 15 June 1965 to be exact, class A4 Pacific No. 60019, 'Bittern', is serviced at Ferryhill shed after working the 0825 three hour express, 'The Grampian', from Glasgow Buchanan Street.

Servicing completed, No. 60019 has backed down to the Joint station where it is seen at platform two heading the 1715 'Granite City' for Glasgow Buchanan Street (where arrival was one minute early at 2014). 'Bittern' survives in preservation, but is not currently in working order.

8

At Aberdeen Joint Station on 11 September 1954, standard class 5 4-6-0 No. 73007 – in spic and span condition and without a trace of leaking steam – heads the 5.30 p.m. 'Granite City' for Glasgow Buchanan Street. Built at Derby Works, it was one of five of the class allocated new to Perth Motive Power Depot in the summer of 1951 and remained there until 1964, being scrapped two years later.

Class A3 Pacific No. 60052, 'Prince Palatine', fires up for a summer Saturday 12.30 p.m. departure from Aberdeen to Edinburgh on 4 July 1964. A racehorse of this name had won the St Leger in 1911.

Class A4 Pacific No. 60026, 'Miles Beevor' (the gentleman had been an LNER director), with the 1.30 p.m. 'Grampian' to Glasgow Buchanan Street via Forfar, and class V2 2-6-2 No. 60835, with the summer Saturday 1.18 p.m. to Glasgow Buchanan Street via Dundee, await departure from Aberdeen on 4 July 1964.

In the days of locomotive hauled trains, pilot engines were employed at both ends of Aberdeen Joint Station for shunting and marshalling of coaching stock. On 5 April 1958 the No. 1, south end, pilot was class N15 0-6-2T No. 69129. The North British Railway had 69 of these locomotives, and a further 30 were added by the LNER, almost exclusively employed in yard shunting and the working of mineral traffic, the principal exception being the banking of passenger trains out of Glasgow Queen Street Station.

Class G5 0-4-4T No. 67327 shunting at the north end of Aberdeen Joint Station on 11 September 1954. Built in 1901 by the North Eastern Railway at Darlington, and transferred to Scotland in 1939 by the LNER, it was scrapped some six months after this photograph was taken.

On 20 August 1955 a former GNSR 4-4-0, No. 62269 of BR class D40, was working as north end pilot. The massive Union Bridge, seen on the right, was engineered by Thomas Telford and opened in 1805 to carry Union Street, the city's main thoroughfare, across the valley of the Denburn.

The Great North station at Waterloo Quay, reached by a one and three-quarter mile branch from the original terminus at Kittybrewster, was used by passengers for only eleven years. However, its continued use for freight traffic included a connection with Aberdeen Corporation gasworks (Scottish Gas Board from 1949) and, on 13 June 1960, I photographed 0-4-0 saddle tank No. 4, named 'Mr Therm' and built by Andrew Barclay & Co. of Kilmarnock in 1947, at Waterloo. For street running its wheels were boxed in.

The spare locomotive at the gasworks was a vintage saddle tank, named 'City of Aberdeen', built by Black, Hawthorn & Co. at Gateshead in 1887. I photographed it at the gasworks on 11 April 1970, on the occasion of a tour for enthusiasts of the surviving harbour lines. It is now to be seen in the SRPS Museum at Bo'ness, West Lothian.

The GNSR had its locomotive works – described by critics as being cramped and inadequate – at Kittybrewster, with the company's main running shed adjoining. On 13 June 1960 class 3F former Caledonian Railway 0-6-0 No. 57644 was photographed on the turntable outside the depot's semi-roundhouse building. Closure (to steam) came a year later. Kittybrewster did not figure largely in my loco-spotting days pre-war, having been dismissed as having 'nae big yins'. In retrospect, the class B12 4-6-0s might well have come within this category.

The Buchan lines from Dyce were opened in stages, being completed to the fishing port of Peterhead in 1862 and reaching Fraserburgh, from a junction at Maud, in 1865. Maud Junction Station features in this photograph, taken on 21 August 1958 and showing standard class 4 2-6-4T No. 80004 running with the 12.25 p.m. train from Aberdeen. As was normal practice, this Fraserburgh-bound train conveyed a portion for Peterhead which was detached here and worked forward by the locomotive, class 2P 4-4-0 No. 40663, waiting at the junction.

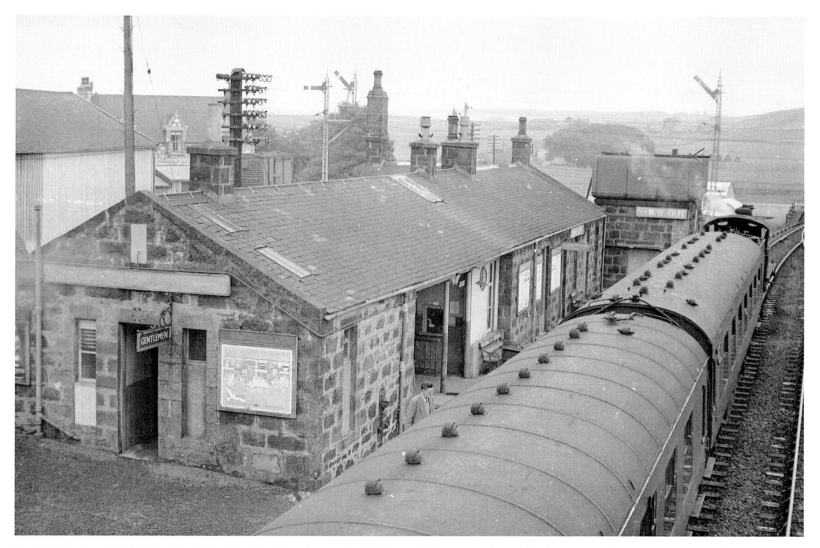

Headed by class 2P 4-4-0 No. 40663, the Peterhead portion of the 12.25 p.m. Buchan train from Aberdeen awaits departure from Maud Junction on 21 August 1958. There were three such workings daily.

Class 2P 4-4-0 No. 40663, photographed on 21 August 1958 at Peterhead, where the station was situated at the back of the town and a lengthy siding gave access to the harbour. The locomotive was with the 3.08 p.m. departure, which it worked to Maud Junction where the coaches were attached to the 3.00 p.m. train from Fraserburgh in order to reach Aberdeen at 4.53 p.m.

Fraserburgh Station was a somewhat fancier affair. On 11 September 1954 standard 2-6-4T No. 80005 was photographed heading the 3.00 p.m. for Aberdeen. Despite introduction of diesel multiple units in 1959, the time-consuming manoeuvrings at Maud, and a shorter mileage by road, brought passenger services on the Buchan lines to an end in 1965.

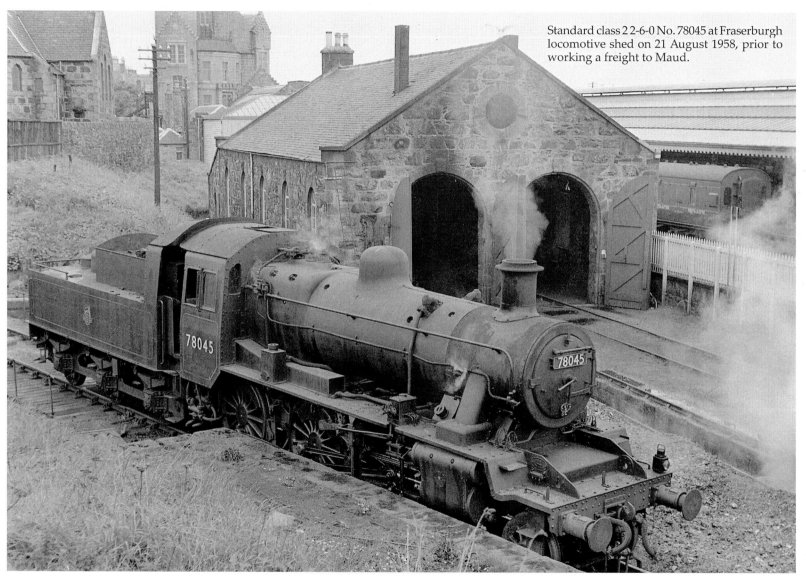

Standard class 2 2-6-0 No. 78045 at Fraserburgh locomotive shed on 21 August 1958, prior to working a freight to Maud.

Fish traffic was, for many years, the mainstay of the Buchan lines, and on 11 September 1954 one such train was seen leaving Fraserburgh for Aberdeen, hauled by class V4 2-6-2 No. 61701 and piloted by standard 2-6-4T No. 80021. With erosion of the fish traffic by road hauliers, complete closure of both the Peterhead and Fraserburgh lines was inevitable, taking place in 1970 and 1979 respectively.

The last line to be built by the Great North of Scotland Railway was the Fraserburgh & St Combs Light Railway. With three intermediate stopping places (two of them 'as required') it was five miles in length and was opened in 1903. Being partly unfenced, it required to be worked by a locomotive fitted with a cowcatcher, such as class 2MT 2-6-0 No. 46460, shown shunting at Fraserburgh on 11 September 1954.

Photographed on 21 August 1958, class 2MT 2-6-0 No. 46460 has arrived at St Combs with the 10.30 a.m. from Fraserburgh, a 23-minute journey, and is running round the train preparatory to working it back to Fraserburgh at 11.15 a.m. Closure under the Beeching era came in 1965.

Class J36 0-6-0 No. 65265, built by the North British Railway in 1892, was photographed, fresh from the paint shop at Inverurie Works, on 13 June 1960. The GNSR locomotive works were originally at Kittybrewster, but construction of large new workshops on a 100-acre site at Inverurie commenced in 1898 and were completed in 1905. Few locomotives were constructed here, however, and, following upon the railway grouping of 1923, only repairs and overhauls were undertaken. The works closed at the end of 1969.

Class Z4 0-4-2T No. 68190 and Z5 No. 68192 – both built by Manning, Wardle & Co. of Leeds in 1915 for the GNSR and intended for the Aberdeen Harbour lines – were photographed on 13 June 1960 while awaiting scrapping at Inverurie Works, having been replaced by diesel shunters.

No. 49, 'Gordon Highlander', on the turntable at Macduff on the occasion of a week's tour of Scotland's railways by English enthusiasts, 13 June 1960. The Macduff branch, 29¾ miles in length, had lost its passenger service in 1951 and the former station can be seen in its elevated site above the town and the North Sea. Freight traffic ended here in 1961, although on the initial section of the branch from Inveramsay to Turriff it continued until 1966.

The penultimate station on the Macduff line was at Banff Bridge and from there it was but a short walk across the River Deveron to Banff harbour where, on 21 August 1958, I photographed the steam collier 'Briardene' discharging a cargo of coal.

From Banff a six-mile branch, dating from 1859, connected at Tillynaught with the coast line from Keith to Elgin. The branch had the doubtful distinction of being the last steam-operated line in the north-east and on 4 July 1964 I photographed standard class 2 2-6-0 No. 78045 calling at Ladysbridge, one of the two intermediate stations, with the 9.50 a.m. from Banff to Tillynaught. This was the last day of passenger services.

Photographed on 4 July 1964, class 2 Mogul No. 78045 awaits departure from Tillynaught with the 7.15 a.m. to Banff.

On 28 August 1959 standard class 4 2-6-4T No. 80021 calls at Portgordon with the coast line portion of the 3.45 p.m. from Aberdeen to Elgin. By this date patronage of the rural lines was declining significantly – only three passengers joined the train on this occasion – and it is hardly surprising that the coast line, formed in 1896 by the joining up of several small companies to form a through route from Keith (Cairnie Junction) to Elgin, was to lose its passenger service in 1968.

The railway reached Keith from Aberdeen in 1856 and there was a locomotive depot there until 1961. On 14 June 1960 I photographed class 3F former Caledonian Railway 0-6-0 No. 57591, one of twelve locomotives on shed that day.

I photographed another of the class 3F 0-6-0s, No. 57634, at Craigellachie on 31 August 1955, as it was about to depart with the 10.10 a.m. train along the Speyside line to Boat of Garten. A sister locomotive, No. 57566, has been preserved and can be seen (as Caledonian Railway No. 828) on the Strathspey Railway at Aviemore. In the background a class B1 4-6-0 is leaving with the 9.30 a.m. from Elgin to Aberdeen.

On 16 June 1962 preserved No. 49, 'Gordon Highlander', and Highland Railway No. 103 made a colourful spectacle as they came off the Speyside line at Craigellachie with the week-long 'Scottish Railtour'. Today, the locomotives remain together in the Glasgow Museum of Transport.

Rothes was an intermediate station between Craigellachie and Elgin with a short-lived connection (closed in 1866) from Orton on the Highland Railway. On 28 August 1959 I photographed standard 2-6-4T No. 80004 arriving at Rothes with the 12.45 p.m. buffet car train from Inverness to Aberdeen.

Black Five 4-6-0 No. 45476 passes the East signal box as it runs into Elgin with the coast portion of the 9.40 a.m. from Aberdeen, 14 June 1960.

At the turn of the century the GNSR station at Elgin was completely rebuilt with three terminal bays and a single long platform connecting with the adjoining Highland Railway station. In a general view of the East station, taken on 31 August 1955, class B1 4-6-0 No. 61400 is heading the 9.30 a.m. to Aberdeen via Craigellachie and sister engine No. 61346 is on the 9.25 a.m. to Aberdeen via the coast.

On an earlier occasion, 11 September 1954, I photographed the 9.25 a.m. from Elgin to Aberdeen with class B1 4-6-0 No. 61352 in charge.

Also photographed at Elgin on 11 September 1954 was class D40 4-4-0 No. 62273, 'George Davidson', acting as station pilot. George Davidson was the last General Manager of the Great North of Scotland Railway.

The following year, on 31 August 1955, a visit to Elgin resulted in a photograph of D40 No. 62264 doing some shunting.

On 28 August 1959 class K2 2-6-0 No. 61792 was photographed at Elgin East with the 5.50 p.m. to Dufftown.

On 28 August 1959 I joined the 2.15 p.m. Aberdeen to Inverness train at Keith Junction and travelled over the former Highland Railway route via Mulben to Elgin West Station, from where the train was reversed into the East station. When I descended there at 4.25 p.m. I had fulfilled my ambition of travelling by steam over every passenger line in Scotland (I had also travelled on a number of freight-only lines). The two stations at Elgin were connected by a lengthy platform and I photographed class B1 4-6-0 No. 61347 steaming through the West station as it resumed its journey to Inverness.

When the coast portion of the 2.15 p.m. train from Aberdeen arrived at Elgin (hauled by standard class 4 2-6-0 No. 76104) on 28 August 1959, its three coaches then formed the 5.11 p.m. to Lossiemouth, worked by standard class 2 2-6-0 No. 78053, which I photographed upon arrival at Lossiemouth. This five and a half mile branch, opened in 1852 as part of the Morayshire Railway, was closed to passengers in 1964 and to freight in 1966.

At Elgin on 28 August 1959 class K2 2-6-0 No. 61782, 'Loch Eil', is turned at the locomotive depot after working in from Keith. Its name was a reminder of earlier days spent on the West Highland line. Diesel shunter No. D2414, seen in the background, was acting as station pilot.

Class 2P 4-4-0 No. 40663, photographed at Elgin shed on 14 June 1960 prior to working a railtour to Forres and Inverness, having been specially cleaned as was usual on such occasions. The class 2P 4-4-0s, built by the LMS in 1928, are probably best remembered for their work on the Glasgow & South Western section.

Black Five No. 45476 calls at the wayside station of Alves on 14 June 1960 with the 12.52 p.m. local train from Elgin to Inverness.

Right: Alves was junction for the Burghead Harbour branch which opened in 1862 and was extended (from a resited station at Burghead) along the coast to Hopeman in 1892. The branch lost its passenger service as early as 1931, while freight traffic over the extension ended in 1957 and between Alves and Burghead in 1966. On 14 June 1960 No. 40663 was photographed upon arrival at Burghead with the railtour mentioned on page 46.

Two years later there was another 'Grand Scottish Tour' by English enthusiasts and, on 16 June 1962, Black Five No. 44978 was photographed going round the triangle at Forres Station with the special train, which included the two restored Caledonian Railway coaches nowadays in the care of the Scottish Railway Preservation Society at Bo'ness.